CONTENTS

CONTENTS...3
CORE EXPECTATIONS FOR PEACE CORPS VOLUNTEERS...........6
PEACE CORPS/UKRAINE HISTORY AND PROGRAMS...................7
History of the Peace Corps in Ukraine...7
History and Future of Peace Corps Programming in Ukraine.............7
COUNTRY OVERVIEW: UKRAINE AT A GLANCE....................8
History..8
Government...9
Economy..10
People and Culture..10

Environment...11
RESOURCES FOR FURTHER INFORMATION............................12
General Information about Ukraine...12
Connect with Returned Volunteers and Other Invitees....................13
Online Articles/Current News Sites about Ukraine..........................13
International Development Sites about Ukraine..............................14
Recommended Books..15
LIVING CONDITIONS AND VOLUNTEER LIFESTYLE................17
Communications...17
Housing and Site Location...18
Living Allowance and Money Management...................................19
Food and Diet..19
Transportation...20
Geography and Climate...21
Social Activities...21
Professionalism, Dress, and Behavior...22
Personal Safety..22
Rewards and Frustrations..23
PEACE CORPS TRAINING..24
Pre-Service Training...24
Technical Training..25
Language Training..26
Health Training..27
Safety Training..28
YOUR HEALTH CARE AND SAFETY IN UKRAINE...................30
Health Issues in Ukraine...30
Helping You Stay Healthy..30
Maintaining Your Health...31

Women's Health Information..32
Your Peace Corps Medical Kit.......................................33
Medical Kit Contents..33
Before Your leave: A Medical Checklist.......................34
Safety and Security- Our Partnership............................35
Support from Staff..39
Crime Data for Ukraine..39
Volunteer Safety Support in Ukraine.............................40
DIVERSITY AND CROSS-CULTURAL ISSUE....................41
Overview of Diversity in Ukraine...................................42
What Might a Volunteer Face?..42
FREQUENTLY ASKED QUESITONS...............................47
WELCOME LETTER FROM UKRAINE VOLUNTEERS.................51
PACKING LIST..56
PRE-DEPARTURE CHECKLIST.....................................61
Family...61
Passport/Travel...62
Medical/Health..62
Insurance..62
Personal Papers...62
Voting..62
Personal Effects...63
Financial Management..63
CONTACTING PEACE CORPS HEADQUARTERS....................64

PEACE CORPS/UKRAINE
HISTORY AND PROGRAMS

History of the Peace Corps in Ukraine

The opening of Peace Corps programs in the Newly Independent States corresponded with the beginning of the end of decades of mistrust and hostility between the United States and the former communist governments in Eastern Europe and the former Soviet Union. In the 21 years that Peace Corps Volunteers have worked in Ukraine, they and their Ukrainian counterparts have faced and overcome a wide range of challenges. Suspicions harbored for years are difficult to overcome. Ambiguity and economic instability have been the norm in Ukraine during the difficult transition to integration with the West. Working and living in a country that is simultaneously deconstructing and reconstructing can often be confusing and frustrating. The Peace Corps has always prided itself on its ability to provide flexible and adaptable Volunteers, and the program in Ukraine truly tests this ability.

The formal agreement establishing Peace Corps/Ukraine was signed in May 1992 in Washington, D.C., by former Ukrainian President Leonid Kravchuk and former U.S. President George Bush. Since the first group of Volunteers arrived in Ukraine in 1992, more than 2,500 Volunteers have worked in the areas of business development, teaching English as a foreign language (TEFL), environmental protection, youth development, and community development. Currently, more than 280 Volunteers work in more than 150 communities throughout the country's 24 provinces and the Autonomous Republic of Crimea.

Peace Corps Volunteers have defined their roles as agents of change, contributing in a variety of ways to the development of Ukraine into a modern European state.

History and Future of Peace Corps Programming in Ukraine

Like conditions in Ukraine, Peace Corps programs here continue to evolve. Today, we have three projects: Community Development, Teaching English as Foreign Language (TEFL) and Youth Development.

Volunteers in the Community Development project enhance local capacities in partnership building, business and management skills, and organizational development. They promote cooperation among three sectors of society— business, government, and nongovernmental organizations (NGOs)—to address local issues of interest to communities. Volunteers in the TEFL project work to expand and improve the quality of English instruction in schools, pedagogical colleges and universities. The Youth Development project addresses the growing gap between the development levels of young people in urban centers and those in rural and otherwise disadvantaged areas who risk falling behind in acquiring the skills and knowledge they will need to succeed.The underlying democratic values of civic engagement, fair play, and optimism that one can create a positive future are the underpinnings of Peace Corps in Ukraine.

COUNTRY OVERVIEW: UKRAINE AT A GLANCE

History

Ukraine, a nation of 45 million people bridging Russia and Western Europe, was deprived of statehood for most of its history – including 700 years as a colony of other Eastern and Central European states (Lithuania and Poland and later Austro-Hungarian and Russian Empires) followed by 70 years of Soviet dictatorship. Today, 21 years after the collapse of the Soviet Union, Ukraine is still struggling to overcome its deep-seated colonial mentality and the authoritarian Soviet legacy based on fear, lack of trust, and repressed initiative

Ukrainians value their country's long and colorful history. Over the centuries, successive civilizations have left their mark on Ukraine – the Scythian, Greek, Scandinavian, Slavic, and Turkic peoples have all had an influence on the culture. The history of the establishment of the Slavic state is rooted in a legend of three brothers and a sister who founded a city along the Dnipro River at the end of the fifth century. Named after one of the brothers, Kyiv became the center of the state of Kyivan-Rus. Kyiv flourished as a center of trade and culture over 1,000 years ago and is the wellspring of the eastern Slavic states that exist today.

The strength of Kyivan-Rus was undermined by infighting between the state's princes, by the sacking of Constantinople by crusaders, and by changes in regional trading patterns. In 1240 the Mongols, led by the grandson of Genghis Khan, attacked Kyiv and subsequently controlled the region for nearly two centuries.

In the wake of Mongol domination, Ukraine was invaded and ruled by Poland, Lithuania, Russia, and others. Cossack armies were formed in response, each led by a hetman (military leader). One of the most famous hetmans in Ukraine's history was Bohdan Khmelnytsky, who inspired an uprising that led to the liberation of Ukraine from Poland in 1648. However, the Treaty of Pereyaslav signed by him in 1654 joined Ukraine and Russia and led to Ukraine's subjugation by the Russian empire and ultimately the Soviet Union.

Joseph Stalin, in an effort to weaken Ukraine further, induced a famine in 1932-1933 by forcibly collecting grain, resulting in the death as many as 10 million Ukrainians by starvation. In September 1941, Ukraine became one of the theaters of World War II when Nazi forces entered Kyiv. In November 1943, Soviet forces recaptured the city, retaining subsequent control of the Ukraine republic for almost 50 years. The world's attention turned to Ukraine in the wake of the Chernobyl nuclear accident in April 1986.

Ukrainians formally realized their dream of independence following the failed coup of August 1991 in Moscow. In a national referendum held on December 1, 1991, Ukrainians endorsed their independence.

Today Ukraine is at a critical point, needing to decide what kind of future it wants for its children, whether it can overcome deep-seated fatalism and its troubled past. Will it become a free society with strong democratic values and rule of law or will it remain a centralized authoritarian state with less freedom, pervasive corruption, massive economic inequality, and a censored press?

Government

Ukraine is governed by a constitution adopted in 1996. The president, who is the head of state, is elected by direct, popular vote for a five-year term and is eligible for a second term. The government is headed by the prime minister, who along with the cabinet is named by president. The unicameral legislature consists of the 450-seat Supreme Council (Verkhovna Rada), whose members are elected to serve five-year terms. Suffrage is granted to all citizens 18 years and older. Administratively, Ukraine is divided into 24 provinces or oblasts, two municipalities with oblast status (Kiev and Sevastopol), and one autonomous republic (Crimea).

Economy

Formerly a major component of the Soviet Union economy , Ukraine experienced a deep recession during the 1990s, including hyperinflation and a drastic fall in economic output. Today, Ukraine is an emerging free market, with a per capita gross domestic product of about US$ 3,800 (2012), fertile agricultural land, and a wealth of raw materials, metals, and natural resources. However, economic freedom continues to be repressed in Ukraine. Previous reforms have failed to promote broad-based economic development or allow the emergence of a more dynamic private sector due to corruption, poor administration of laws and deficiencies in contract enforcement and protection of property rights.

People and Culture

The richness of Ukraine's culture reflects its history as a crossing point and meeting ground for European and Asian cultures and peoples. While 75 percent of the population is Ukrainian, more than 110 other ethnic groups are represented in the country. Among the numerous faiths practiced in Ukraine are Ukrainian Orthodoxy, Ukrainian Catholicism, Protestantism, Judaism, and Islam.

Ukrainian was declared the official language at independence in 1991, though Russian and Ukrainian are also official languages in Crimea. While Ukrainian is most often heard in western Ukraine and in smaller towns and villages, Russian is the primary language spoken by many people in large cities, particularly in the eastern and southern part of the country. In recent years, there have been tensions between the Ukrainian- and Russian-speaking segments of the population. Reflecting the diversity of the population, some Ukrainians also speak Romanian, Hungarian, or Polish.

Environment

Ukraine is a beautiful country with a rich variety of natural resources, including about 70,000 species of flora and fauna and nearly 8,000 deposits of 94 minerals of commercial value.

A small part of the country is mountainous, with the highest peak being Hoverla (2,061 meters) in the Carpathian Mountains. Mixed forests cover the north. The middle of the country consists of a mosaic of forests and steppe, and the south consists of steppe, restricted forests, and wetlands. Ukraine has significant environmental problems, resulting from the Chernobyl nuclear power plant disaster in 1986 and from industrial pollution.

RESOURCES FOR FURTHER INFORMATION

Following is a list of websites for additional information about the Peace Corps and Ukraine and to connect you to returned Volunteers and other invitees. Please keep in mind that although we try to make sure all these links are active and current, we cannot guarantee it. If you do not have access to the Internet, visit your local library. Libraries offer free Internet usage and often let you print information to take home.

A note of caution: As you surf the Internet, be aware that you may find bulletin boards and chat rooms in which people are free to express opinions about the Peace Corps based on their own experience, including comments by those who were unhappy with their choice to serve in the Peace Corps. These opinions are not those of the Peace Corps or the U.S. government, and we hope you will keep in mind that no two people experience their service in the same way.

General Information About Ukraine

www.countrywatch.com/

On this site, you can learn anything from what time it is in the capital of Ukraine to how to convert from the dollar to the Ukraine currency. Just click on Ukraine and go from there.

www.lonelyplanet.com/destinations

Visit this site for general travel advice about almost any country in the world.

www.state.gov

The State Department's website issues background notes periodically about countries around the world. Find *Ukraine* and learn more about its social and political history. You can also go to the site's international travel section to check on conditions that may affect your safety.

www.geography.about.com/library/maps/blindex.htm

This online world atlas includes maps and geographical information, and each country page contains links to other sites, such as the Library of Congress, that contain comprehensive historical, social, and political background.

www.cyberschoolbus.un.org

This United Nations site allows you to search for statistical information for member states of the U.N.

www.worldinformation.org

This site provides an additional source of current and historical information about countries around the world.

Connect With Returned Volunteers and Other Invitees

www.peacecorpsconnect.org

This is the site of the National Peace Corps Association, made up of returned Volunteers. On this site you can find links to all the Web pages of the ─Friends of'' groups for most countries of service, comprised of former Volunteers who served in those countries. There are also regional groups that frequently get together for social events and local volunteer activities. Or go straight to the Friends of **Ukraine** site: http://groups.yahoo.com/group/FriendsOfUkraine/

www.PeaceCorpsWorldwide.org

This site is hosted by a group of returned Volunteer writers. It is a monthly online publication of essays and Volunteer accounts of their Peace Corps service.

Online Articles/Current News Sites About Ukraine

www.brama.com/news

This site offers substantive and timely information about Ukraine and links to complementary services.

http://ukrainianweek.com/

This site of the Ukrainian Weekly Magazine has both daily news and analytical articles in English.

http://www.kyivpost.com/

The *Kyiv Post*, an informative source of English-language news on Ukraine, includes comprehensive statistics and weekly summaries of developments in key industries. Subscribers receive a daily email with summaries of what the local press is writing about.

www.ukraine-today.com

Aimed at business travelers, this site offers interesting and useful information for visitors to Ukraine.

International Development Sites About Ukraine

www.usukraine.org

U.S.-Ukraine Foundation

www.usaid.gov/where-we-work/europe-and-eurasia/ukraine

U.S. Agency for International Development in Ukraine

http://kiev.usembassy.gov

U.S. Embassy in Kyiv

http://www.un.org.ua/

United Nations in Kyiv

www.worldbank.org.ua

World Bank in Ukraine

Recommended Books

1. Dolot, Miron. *Execution by Hunger: The Hidden Holocaust*. New York: W.W. Norton, 1987.

A description of the forced collectivization of Russian agriculture in 1929-1931 and the ensuing famine in Ukraine.

2. Subtelny, Orest. *Ukraine: A History, 4th Edition*. University of Toronto Press, 2009.

A very broad, comprehensive and readable history of Ukraine.

3. Timothy Snyder. *Bloodlands: Europe Between Hitler and Stalin*. New York: Basic Books, 2012.

Bloodlands is a new kind of European history, presenting the mass murders committed by the Nazi and Stalinist regimes as two aspects of a single history, in the time and place where they occurred: between Germany and Russia, when Hitler and Stalin both held power.

4. Nebesky, Richard. *Russia, Ukraine, and Belarus*. London: Lonely Planet, 1996.

An excellent guidebook for travelers on history, culture, security, bureaucracy, transportation, hotels, and restaurants in the cities of Russia and Ukraine.

5. Reid, Anna. *Borderland: A Journey Through the History of Ukraine.* Boulder, Colo.: Westview Press, 2000.

Combining historical research with travel and interviews with peasants and politicians, rabbis and racketeers, dissidents and paramilitaries, and survivors of Stalin's famine and of Nazi labor camps, Reid charts Ukraine's tragic past and explores its struggle to build a national future.

6. Wilson, Andrew. *The Ukrainians: Unexpected Nation* (2nd ed.). New Haven, Conn.: Yale University Press, 2002.

A comprehensive source of information about Ukraine and its people. The author discusses relations between Ukraine and Russia and analyzes the issues of identity, culture, and religion in Ukraine since its independence in 1991.

Books About the History of the Peace Corps

1. Hoffman, Elizabeth Cobbs. *All You Need is Love: The Peace Corps and the Spirit of the 1960s.* Cambridge, Mass.: Harvard University Press, 2000.

2. Rice, Gerald T. *The Bold Experiment: JFK's Peace Corps.* Notre Dame, Ind.: University of Notre Dame Press, 1985.

3. Stossel, Scott. *Sarge: The Life and Times of Sargent Shriver.* Washington, D.C.: Smithsonian Institution Press, 2004.

4. Meisler, Stanley. *When the World Calls: The Inside Story of the Peace Corps and its First 50 Years.* Boston, Mass.: Beacon Press, 2011.

Books on the Volunteer Experience

1. Dirlam, Sharon. *Beyond Siberia: Two Years in a Forgotten Place.* Santa Barbara, Calif.: McSeas Books, 2004.

2. Casebolt, Marjorie DeMoss. *Margarita: A Guatemalan Peace Corps Experience.* Gig Harbor, Wash.: Red Apple Publishing, 2000.

3. Erdman, Sarah. *Nine Hills to Nambonkaha: Two Years in the Heart of an African Village.* New York, N.Y.: Picador, 2003.

4. Hessler, Peter. *River Town: Two Years on the Yangtze*. New York, N.Y.: Perennial, 2001.

5. Kennedy, Geraldine ed. *From the Center of the Earth: Stories out of the Peace Corps.* Santa Monica, Calif.: Clover Park Press, 1991.

6. Thompsen, Moritz. *Living Poor: A Peace Corps Chronicle*. Seattle, Wash.: University of Washington Press, 1997 (reprint).

LIVING CONDITIONS AND VOLUNTEER LIFESTYLE

Communications

Only small, flat envelopes (no boxes, pouches, or packages) can be delivered to trainess over the course of pre-service training. Because Peace Corps/Ukraine cannot be responsible for property mailed to trainees, delivery of boxes and packages sent to this address will be declined. Mail takes a minimum of two weeks to arrive in Ukraine.

Your address during training will be:

U.S. Peace Corps/Ukraine
PCT (Name of Trainee)
P.O. Box 204
01032
Kyiv, Ukraine

Once you become a Volunteer and move to your permanent site, you may receive mail there, either at a post office box or at your office. Family and friends should not mail you valuable items, as mail sometimes arrives opened, with items missing, or does not arrive at all. Airmail is more reliable, but more expensive, than surface mail. A number of international mail services operate in Ukraine, including UPS and DHL.

Telecommunications in Ukraine lags far behind that in the United States. Many Ukrainians do not have their own land lines, and it is possible that you will not have one. Practically all Ukrainians use cellular phones. Peace Corps/Ukraine discourages you from bringing a cellphone from home because it is highly unlikely that a cellular plan in the United States will cover Ukraine. You will receive a special allowance of about $30 to buy a cheap cellphone in Ukraine. All incoming calls are free of charge.

Computers may not be available at your workplace, and many Volunteers find that having their own is helpful. Although some Volunteers have purchased laptops in Ukraine, the selection is limited and generally more expensive than in the U.S. If you decide to bring a laptop, make sure you bring the necessary power converter, surge protection, and plug adapter. The Peace Corps encourages you to insure your computer against theft.

Volunteers are expected to adhere to high standards of discretion when expressing their impressions and opinions about the countries where they serve. Blogs are easily accessible to anyone with an Internet connection and so any offensive content that is posted on a blog can be accessed by your host country colleagues, friends, and general public. Therefore, in addition to ensuring that the content is appropriate and culturally sensitive, Volunteers are urged to password protect their blogs in order to guarantee that the blog is accessed only by the audience intended by the Volunteer. Additional information about blogs will be given during pre-service training (PST).

Housing and Site Location

Your living conditions in Ukraine will require some adjustments to your lifestyle.

Volunteers in Ukraine live in a wide range of sites, from medium-sized cities (about 20 percent), to small towns or villages with few modern amenities (about 80 percent). You will be assigned a site during training after providing input on your site preferences. However, many factors influence the site identification process, including the needs of the host community, and the Peace Corps cannot guarantee placement where you would ideally like to be.

During training, you will stay with a host family to enhance your language learning, cultural integration and safety. For many Volunteers, homestays will extend beyond training and last throughout their two-year assignments. Independent housing is scarce and not guaranteed. Other housing options include a dormitory or a modest apartment provided by your worksite.

You will be provided with most of the furnishings you need, along with a settling-in allowance for additional items. Your regional manager will work with you and your Ukrainian counterpart to ensure that you can obtain necessities.

Many towns have to ration water and electricity, and hot water may not be available. Ukrainians usually keep buckets of water and candles available.

Heat in towns and cities is centrally controlled and is turned on and off according to finances and the calendar, not the weather. Volunteers are issued space heaters when they move to their sites. In some communities Volunteers are expected to heat their houses using a wood or coal-burning stove.

Living Allowance and Money Management

As a Volunteer, you will receive several allowances. Your monthly living allowance is intended to cover your basic living expenses; food, household supplies, clothing, recreation, transportation, reading material, and other incidentals. It is reviewed every year through a market survey to ensure that it is adequate. Currently it is roughly equivalent to $170, which is transferred into each Volunteer's local bank account. Another allowance is for in-country travel and is based on a set number of round trips from your site to Kyiv and includes lodging and per diem. You will also receive a monthly vacation allowance of $24. Finally, when you move into your permanent housing at site, you will receive a one-time settling-in allowance to buy basic household items.

The Peace Corps discourages you from supplementing your income with money brought from home while in Ukraine. Volunteers are expected to live at the same level as their Ukrainian colleagues.

Food and Diet

During training, your host family will provide you with most meals, so you will have plenty of opportunities to become familiar with Ukrainian food. As in many countries, the availability of certain foods depends on the season, with a wider range of vegetables and fruits available in the spring and summer. Many Volunteers enjoy learning how to preserve and can food for the winter, as do many Ukrainians. The Ukrainian diet relies heavily on meat (mostly pork and chicken), potatoes, beets, onions, and cabbage in the winter.

The traditional diet can be high in fat and cholesterol. Vegetarians may find it challenging to maintain their usual diet because of the lack of fruits and vegetables at certain times of the year. Still, there are many types of Ukrainian salads, consisting of cabbage, beets, carrots, and other seasonal and year-round vegetables. In addition, an increasing number of soy products are being imported from Europe.

Grocery stores similar to those in the US are appearing all over Ukraine, but most PCVs shop in open-air markets and small shops that sell produce and all the other necessities of life, from wonderful black bread and vegetables to live chickens and clothing. These bazaars allow you to taste many items before purchasing them. It is unlikely you will find fresher products anywhere else and they open early so you can shop before you go to work for the day.

Transportation

Ukraine has a very well-developed public transportation system of public transportation. Every large city and regional capital is connected to the extensive national railway network.Buses and minibuses operate between shorter distances. Many of the trains are overnight trains, so Volunteers can leave their sites at night and arrive at their destinations in the morning. An alternative that is gaining popularity is a luxury bus network, which also provides service to many cities.

Most cities and towns in Ukraine have a comprehensive public transportation system of buses, trolleys and trams;Kyiv, Kharkov and Dnipropetrovsk have subways. Public transportation is efficient and inexpensive, but vehicles can be very old and very crowded. In addition to taxi services, most cities have direct-route taxis that look like vans. In towns and villages without public transportation, people get around by bicycles and on foot.

Roads in Ukraine are in generally poor condition. Given the state of roads and the weather conditions, travel between cities by buses and vans at night and in the winter can be particularly treacherous.

During pre-service training you will have an opportunity to familiarize yourself with the public transportation system in Ukraine and learn how to navigate in your training community. In Kyiv, you will learn where to buy tickets and how to choose the safest and reliable travel option.

Geography and Climate

Ukraine is situated between 44 and 52 degrees latitude in the continental temperate zone in Eastern Europe and has an area of 603,000 km^2. It borders Belarus on the north, Poland, Slovakia, Hungary, Romania, and Moldova on the west, and Russia on the East. Ukraine's time zone is 2 hours ahead of London, 7 hours ahead of New York City and 10 hours ahead of Los Angeles.

Ukraine is a mostly flat country with mountains only on the Crimean peninsula in the west. Ukraine has many rivers — the Dnipro (Dniepr), Pivdennyy Buh ("Southern Buh"), Dnister, Siverskyy Donets, Desna, Dunay (Danube), and many others — and its southern border is washed by the Black Sea, which connects to the Mediterranean Sea through Turkey.

Ukraine has a continental climate, with the exception of the southern coast of Crimea, which is in a subtropical zone. Although many people imagine Ukraine as a country of snow and ice, it has four distinct seasons, with summer temperatures averaging in the 70s and 80s.

Winters in Ukraine are long and cold, and as a result of its northern latitude, daylight in the winter is limited. Some Volunteers with a history of seasonal affective disorder or depression have found the limited exposure to sunlight to be an added challenge of service in Ukraine.

Social Activities

The life of a Volunteer is filled with learning and networking 24 hours a day, seven days a week. Having a cup of tea with a Ukrainian neighbor is as much a part of the Volunteer experience as teaching a class or seminar. Social activities will vary depending on where you live and might include taking part in local festivals, parties, and dances. In addition, although the Peace Corps encourages Volunteers to remain at their sites as an essential strategy for integrating into their communities, some Volunteers occasionally visit nearby Volunteers on weekends. Most towns and cities have cafes and restaurants for evenings out, and some Volunteers have older model televisions in their apartments.

Professionalism, Dress, and Behavior

The Peace Corps expects you to behave in a way that will foster respect toward you in your community and reflect well on the Peace Corps and on the United States. You will receive an orientation to appropriate behavior and cultural sensitivity during training. As a Volunteer, you have the status of an invited guest and thus must be sensitive to the habits, tastes, and taboos of your Ukrainian hosts. You need to be aware that behavior that jeopardizes the Peace Corps' mission in Ukraine or your personal safety will not be tolerated and could lead to administrative separation, a decision by the Peace Corps to terminate your service.

All Volunteers were invited to serve in a professional capacity. Personal appearance is very important in Ukraine, and dressing professionally helps PCVs gain trust and credibility. For women, professional attire includes dress pants or skirts paired with blouses or sweaters, or dresses, paired with dress shoes. Although the majority of Ukrainian women wear high heels, flats are also appropriate. For men, dress slacks or khakis paired with sweaters, polo or Oxford shirts are appropriate. A jacket and tie are usually not required for daily wear, however they are important to have for more formal occasions. It is also important that clothes be clean and ironed, and that shoes are kept clean and polished. Ukraine styles are somewhat different than in the United States, but clothing acceptable as business or professional dress in the US will be accepted as such in Ukraine.

Personal Safety

More detailed information about the Peace Corps' approach to safety is contained in the "Health Care and Safety" chapter, but it is an important issue and cannot be overemphasized. As stated in the *Volunteer Handbook*, becoming a Peace Corps Volunteer entails certain safety risks. Living and traveling in an unfamiliar environment (oftentimes alone), having a limited understanding of local language and culture, and being perceived as well-off are some of the factors that can put a Volunteer at risk. Many Volunteers experience varying degrees of unwanted attention and harassment. Petty thefts and burglaries are not uncommon, and incidents of physical and sexual assault do occur, although most Ukraine Volunteers complete their two years of service without incident. The Peace Corps has established procedures and policies designed to help you reduce your risks and enhance your safety and security. These procedures and policies, in addition to safety training, will be provided once you arrive in Ukraine. Using these tools, you are expected to take responsibility for your safety and well-being.

Each staff member at the Peace Corps is committed to providing Volunteers with the support they need to successfully meet the challenges they will face to have a safe, healthy, and productive service. We encourage Volunteers and families to look at our safety and security information on the Peace Corps website at www.peacecorps.gov/safety.

Information on these pages gives messages on Volunteer health and Volunteer safety. There is a section titled —Safety and Security —Our Partnership." Among topics addressed are the risks of serving as a Volunteer, posts' safety support systems, and emergency planning and communications.

Rewards and Frustrations

You can expect it will take time for your Ukrainian counterparts to understand your role as a Volunteer and for you to determine your appropriate responsibilities. You may not be stepping into a well-defined situation. You will need to remember that you are part of a long-term development project. A challenge throughout your assignment will be to help your colleagues develop their capacity to continue to perform similar work after your departure.

You may be frustrated at times by not being proficient in the local language, even after the pre-service training. While your counterpart may have some command of English, most of your colleagues will not. Learning Ukrainian or Russian will make a major difference in your work, in your ability to adapt to living in Ukraine, and in your appreciation of Ukrainian society and culture.

To have a successful experience as a Volunteer, you must be motivated, flexible, and willing to work hard. You will need to identify local resources and institutions with which you can cooperate. To be effective, you might need to —unlearn" practices that you have developed on the basis of prior experiences. Despite these challenges—or perhaps because of them— Volunteers in Ukraine find satisfaction in demonstrating to their colleagues that every individual can make a difference in the creation of a civil society. As it has in the past, Ukraine is poised to play a pivotal role in the future of Europe and the world. Volunteers have a unique opportunity to impact the nature of that role.

PEACE CORPS TRAINING

Overview of Pre-Service Training

Pre-service training (PST) is the first event within a competency-based training program that continues throughout your 27 months of service in Ukraine. It ensures that Volunteers are equipped with the knowledge, skills, and attitudes to effectively perform their jobs.

PST lasts approximately 11 weeks and is conducted in Ukraine and facilitated by training and programming staff and current Volunteers with participation from representatives of Ukraine organizations. You will need to meet learning objectives and successfully achieve competencies, including language standards, to swear in as a Peace Corps Volunteer.

Peace Corps training is founded on adult learning methods and includes experiential –hands-on" applications such as conducting a participatory community needs assessment and facilitating groups.

use a Peace Corps Ukraine uses a community-based model of PST. Your entire training group will meet only for the initial orientation (Arrival Retreat), for several days in the middle of PST (PST University), and then at the end of PST (Transition to Service Conference). For most of the PST however, groups of 4-5 trainees will live in towns and villages located within two-to three-hour ride from Kyiv. Each group will have a language and cross-cultural facilitator and a technical and cultural facilitator (the latter will be shared by every two between two groups).

Successful sustainable development work is based on the local trust and confidence Volunteers build by living in, and respectfully integrating into, the Ukraine community and culture. Trainees are prepared for this through a –homestay" experience. Staying with a Ukrainian family not only facilitates your integration into the community, but it fosters language learning and cross-cultural acceptance and trust, which help ensure your health, safety, and security.

As a trainee, you will play an active role in self-education. The success of your learning will be enhanced by your own effort to take responsibility for your learning and through sharing experiences with others.

Technical Training

Technical training will prepare you to work in Ukraine by building on the skills you already have and helping you develop new skills in a manner appropriate to the needs of the country. The Peace Corps staff, Ukraine experts, and current Volunteers will conduct the training program. Training places great emphasis on learning how to transfer the skills you have to the community in which you will serve as a Volunteer.

Technical training will include sessions on the general economic and political environment in Ukraine and strategies for working within such a framework. You will review your technical sector's goals and will meet with the Ukrainian agencies and organizations that invited the Peace Corps to assist them. You will be supported and evaluated throughout the training to build the confidence and skills you need to undertake your project activities and be a productive member of your community.

Starting from Week 1, you will participate in on-going PST internship activities:

- **Youth Development:** You will be assigned to secondary schools or centers of social services for youth and will observe and teach healthy life styles and civics classes, assist English teachers and prepare and facilitate youth club meetings. You will visit departments of youth and sport, children's creativity centers, orphanages and other partner organizations .Finally, together with your community partners, you will organize and run a 3-day youth camp and design and implement a community project to address local needs.

- **Community Development**: You will have meetings with the local government administrations, NGO leaders and other community partners. You will be involved in activities similar to what you will do at your sites, such as community mapping, needs assessment, professional meetings and trainings. Finally, together with community members, you will design and implement community projects to address community needs.

- **TEFL:** You will be assigned to schools and universities and will be involved in lesson observations and analysis, designing lesson plans, teaching, working with Ukrainian teachers, devising strategies for classroom management, and organizing extra-curricular activities, including an English Language Club for your students and a community/ school project.

Language Training

As a Peace Corps Volunteer, you will find that language skills are key to personal and professional satisfaction during your service. These skills are critical to your job performance, they help you integrate into your community, and they can ease your personal adaptation to the new surroundings. Therefore, language training is at the heart of the training program. You must successfully meet minimum language requirements to complete training and become a Volunteer. Ukrainian language instructors teach formal language classes five days a week in small groups of four to five people.

Your language training will incorporate a community-based approach. In addition to classroom time, you will be given assignments to work on outside of the classroom and with your host family. The goal is to get you to a point of basic social communication skills so you can practice and develop language skills further once you are at your site. Prior to being sworn in as a Volunteer, you will work on strategies to continue language studies during your service.

You will have language classes (either Ukrainian or Russian) conducted by your Language/Cultural Facilitator (LCF) Monday through Friday four to five hours a day, including classroom instruction, language field trips, self-directed learning activities, technical language and tutoring. The daily schedule of your language classes should be agreed upon by your group and your LCF, taking into account your technical training and internship activities. Classes will generally take place at your LCF's residence.

During PST you will be focusing on one local language (either Ukrainian or Russian) and introduced to the other one, as both languages are spoken in Ukraine. While the official state language is Ukrainian, you may hear a lot of Russian in many cities and towns of southern, eastern, and northern Ukraine. The percentage of Ukrainian spoken on the street is about 30% in Kyiv, 50-60% in Zhytomyr, Vinnytsya, and Khmelnytskyy, 5-10% in Kharkiv and Donetsk, 1-5% in Crimea, and 80-95% in Western Ukraine. Rural areas have a higher concentration of Ukrainian speakers.

We strongly encourage you to continue language learning after PST by taking tutoring classes at your site and participating in Peace Corps language refreshers and camps.

Cross-Cultural Training

As part of your pre-service training, you will live with a Ukrainian host family. This experience is designed to ease your transition to life at your site. Families go through an orientation conducted by Peace Corps staff to explain the purpose of pre-service training and to assist them in helping you adapt to living in Ukraine. Many Volunteers form strong and lasting friendships with their host families.

Cross-cultural and community development training will help you improve your communication skills and understand your role as a facilitator of development. You will be exposed to topics such as community mobilization, conflict resolution, gender and development, nonformal and adult education strategies, and political structures.

For some of you, this is your first experience with cross-cultural training. For others, it may be reinforcement. To make the best use of your time, PST will focus on the essential information necessary for understanding Ukraine and Ukrainians and the skills you need for successful cultural adjustment to your new environment and productive intercultural interactions.

You will learn that culture is a generalization about groups of people's behaviors, and consequently, cross-cultural training is a generalized solution. And when we deal with generalizations there are always exceptions. The secret of cross-cultural success is awareness. If you are aware of how culture influences thought and behavior, how people from other cultures may see you, and how your cultural background may influence how you see them - then deeper understanding comes easier.

Your patience and your ability to stay positive and open to new experiences, as well as an ability to laugh at yourself, will be crucial to your success.

Both your LCF and TCF will facilitate your adjustment to the new culture and realities of life in Ukraine.

Health Training

During pre-service training, you will be given basic medical training and information. You will be expected to practice preventive health care and to take responsibility for your own health by adhering to all medical policies. Trainees are required to attend all medical sessions. The topics include preventive health measures and minor and major medical issues that you might encounter while in Ukraine. Nutrition, mental health, setting up a safe living compound, and how to avoid HIV/AIDS and other sexually transmitted diseases (STDs) are also covered.

The health of the Trainees and Volunteers is of paramount importance. There are several Peace Corps Medical Officers (PCMOs) in Ukraine. They are responsible for informing Trainees about ways to stay healthy, giving inoculations, discussing medical issues, routine diagnoses, and arranging for your health care in Ukraine.

During the Arrival Retreat you will have an interview with one of our PCMOs and discuss any personal health concerns you might have.

During PST, PCMOs will travel to your training communities to conduct two Personal Health Days (with a focus on physical and mental health).

Safety Training

During the safety training sessions, you will learn how to adopt a lifestyle that reduces your risks at home, at work, and during your travels. You will also learn appropriate, effective strategies for coping with unwanted attention and about your individual responsibility for promoting safety throughout your service.

The safety and security of Trainees and Volunteers in Ukraine is the number one priority of all Peace Corps Staff. Peace Corps Ukraine's Safety and Security Coordinator is responsible for developing safety and security related materials, presenting information, tracking safety incidents, reacting in case of emergency issues, dealing with the local police and other safety and security related tasks.

Personal Safety training will be facilitated both by the Safety and Security Coordinator and Language/Cross-Cultural Facilitators. During Personal Safety training, you will gain understanding of how Ukrainians interpret signals, and how you could adjust your sound judgment and safety skills to Ukrainian realities. You will learn how not to put yourself in danger and how to get out of potentially unsafe situations. Remember: Safety training is not only about avoiding criminal situations – it's about your lifestyle and cultural adjustment.

Additional Trainings During Volunteer Service

In its commitment to institutionalize quality training, the Peace Corps has implemented a training system that provides Volunteers with continual opportunities to examine their commitment to Peace Corps service while increasing their technical and cross-cultural skills. During service, there are usually three training events. The titles and objectives for those trainings are as follows:

- In-service training: *Provides an opportunity for Volunteers to upgrade their technical, language, and project development skills while sharing their experiences and reaffirming their commitment after having served for three to six months.*

- Midterm conference (done in conjunction with technical sector in-service): *Assists Volunteers in reviewing their first year, reassessing their personal and project objectives, and planning for their second year of service.*

- Close-of-service conference: *Prepares Volunteers for the future after Peace Corps service and reviews their respective projects and personal experiences.*

The number, length, and design of these trainings are adapted to country-specific needs and conditions. The key to the training system is that training events are integrated and interrelated, from the pre-departure orientation through the end of your service, and are planned, implemented, and evaluated cooperatively by the training staff, Peace Corps staff, and Volunteers.

YOUR HEALTH CARE AND
SAFETY IN UKRAINE

The Peace Corps' highest priority is maintaining the good health and safety of every Volunteer. Peace Corps medical programs emphasize the preventive, rather than the curative, approach to disease. The Peace Corps in Ukraine maintains a clinic with a full-time medical officer, who takes care of Volunteers' primary health care needs. Additional medical services, such as testing and basic treatment, are also available in Ukraine at local hospitals. If you become seriously ill, you will be transported either to an American-standard medical facility in the region or to the United States.

Health Issues in Ukraine

Radiation and nuclear safety. The U.S. Department of Energy and the Ukrainian Nuclear Regulatory Commission collaborate in monitoring and ensuring safety at all operating nuclear power plants in Ukraine. Volunteers are not placed within 30 kilometers of such facilities. The effects of the 1986 Chernobyl accident continue to be monitored. No Volunteers are placed at any site with higher-than-normal levels of radiation. The Ukrainian government monitors the level of radiation in fresh foods and meats sold in Ukraine.

Industrial and air pollution. During the Soviet era, the central and eastern regions of Ukraine were heavily industrialized, resulting in air, ground and water pollution. Volunteers are not placed in sites with unacceptable levels of pollution. While smog in cities may be no worse than in the United States, Volunteers with asthma may find their condition exacerbated.

Insufficient infrastructure. Water supply systems in some communities do not guarantee potable water. In other locations, availability of water is limited to several hours. Hot water and heating are often not available and residents may use space heaters, coal- or wood-burning stoves, or other means to heat their homes. In general, living quarters in the winter are cooler than what Americans are accustomed to.

Helping You Stay Healthy

The Peace Corps will provide you with all the necessary inoculations, medications, and information to stay healthy. Upon your arrival in Ukraine, you will receive a medical handbook. At the end of training, you will receive a medical kit with supplies to take care of mild illnesses and first aid needs. The contents of the kit are listed later in this chapter.

During pre-service training, you will have access to basic medical supplies through the medical officer. However, you will be responsible for your own supply of prescription drugs and any other specific medical supplies you require, as the Peace Corps will not order these items during training. Please bring a three-month supply of any prescription drugs you use, since they may not be available here and it may take several months for shipments to arrive.

You will have physicals at midservice and at the end of your service. If you develop a serious medical problem during your service, the medical officer in Ukraine will consult with the Office of Medical Services in Washington, D.C. If it is determined that your condition cannot be treated in Ukraine, you may be sent out of the country for further evaluation and care.

Maintaining Your Health

As a Volunteer, you must accept considerable responsibility for your own health. Proper precautions will significantly reduce your risk of serious illness or injury. The adage –An ounce of prevention …" becomes extremely important in areas where diagnostic and treatment facilities are not up to the standards of the United States. The most important of your responsibilities in Ukraine is to take the following preventive measures:

- Limit your consumption of alcohol as it damages your health and decreases immunity. PCVs are often in social situations that involve alcohol and should be prepared to deal with the pressure to drink.

- Be aware of the emotional health challenges that exist during the dark winter months in Ukraine. PCVs that have a history of Seasonal Affective Disorder or depression should be aware and take measures to prepare.

- Be prepared to be actively aware of the food you eat to reduce exposure to food-borne maladies, including watching what you eat and drink, making sure raw food is cleaned, and regularly washing your hands.

Many illnesses that afflict Volunteers worldwide are entirely preventable if proper food and water precautions are taken. These illnesses include food poisoning, parasitic infections, hepatitis A, dysentery, Guinea worms, tapeworms, and typhoid fever. Your medical officer will discuss specific standards for water and food preparation in Ukraine during pre-service training.

Abstinence is the only certain choice for preventing infection with HIV and other sexually transmitted diseases. You are taking risks if you choose to be sexually active. To lessen risk, use a condom every time you have sex. Whether your partner is a host country citizen, a fellow Volunteer, or anyone else, do not assume this person is free of HIV/AIDS or other STDs. You will receive more information from the medical officer about this important issue.

Volunteers are expected to adhere to an effective means of birth control to prevent an unplanned pregnancy. Your medical officer can help you decide on the most appropriate method to suit your individual needs. Contraceptive methods are available without charge from the medical officer.

It is critical to your health that you promptly report to the medical office or other designated facility for scheduled immunizations, and that you let the medical officer know immediately of significant illnesses and injuries.

Women's Health Information

Pregnancy is treated in the same manner as other Volunteer health conditions that require medical attention but also have programmatic ramifications. The Peace Corps is responsible for determining the medical risk and the availability of appropriate medical care if the Volunteer remains in-country. Given the circumstances under which Volunteers live and work in Peace Corps countries, it is rare that the Peace Corps' medical and programmatic standards for continued service during pregnancy can be met.

If feminine hygiene products are not available for you to purchase on the local market, the Peace Corps medical officer in Ukraine will provide them. If you require a specific product, please bring a three-month supply with you.

Your Peace Corps Medical Kit

The Peace Corps medical officer will provide you with a kit that contains basic items necessary to prevent and treat illnesses that may occur during service. Kit items can be periodically restocked at the medical office.

Medical Kit Contents

Ace bandages

Adhesive tape

American Red Cross First Aid & Safety Handbook

Antacid tablets (Tums)

Antibiotic ointment (Bacitracin/Neomycin/Polymycin B)

Antiseptic antimicrobial skin cleaner (Hibiclens)

Band-Aids

Butterfly closures

Calamine lotion

Cepacol lozenges

Condoms

Dental floss

Diphenhydramine HCL 25 mg (Benadryl)

Insect repellent stick (Cutter's)

Iodine tablets (for water purification)

Lip balm (Chapstick)

Oral rehydration salts

Oral thermometer (Fahrenheit)

Pseudoephedrine HCL 30 mg (Sudafed)

Robitussin-DM lozenges (for cough)

Scissors

Sterile gauze pads

Tetrahydrozaline eyedrops (Visine)

Tinactin (antifungal cream)

Tweezers

Before You Leave: A Medical Checklist

If there has been any change in your health—physical, mental, or dental—since you submitted your examination reports to the Peace Corps, you must immediately notify the Office of Medical Services. Failure to disclose new illnesses, injuries, allergies, or pregnancy can endanger your health and may jeopardize your eligibility to serve.

If your dental exam was done more than a year ago, or if your physical exam is more than two years old, contact the Office of Medical Services to find out whether you need to update your records. If your dentist or Peace Corps dental consultant has recommended that you undergo dental treatment or repair, you must complete that work and make sure your dentist sends requested confirmation reports or X-rays to the Office of Medical Services.

If you wish to avoid having duplicate vaccinations, contact your physician's office to obtain a copy of your immunization record and bring it to your pre-departure orientation. If you have any immunizations prior to Peace Corps service, the Peace Corps cannot reimburse you for the cost. The Peace Corps will provide all the immunizations necessary for your overseas assignment, either at your pre-departure orientation or shortly after you arrive in Ukraine. You do not need to begin taking malaria medication prior to departure.

Bring a three-month supply of any prescription or over-the-counter medication you use on a regular basis, including birth control pills. Although the Peace Corps cannot reimburse you for this three-month supply, it will order refills during your service. While awaiting shipment—which can take several months—you will be dependent on your own medication supply. The Peace Corps will not pay for herbal or nonprescribed medications, such as St. John's wort, glucosamine, selenium, or antioxidant supplements.

You are encouraged to bring copies of medical prescriptions signed by your physician. This is not a requirement, but they might come in handy if you are questioned in transit about carrying a three-month supply of prescription drugs.

If you wear eyeglasses, bring two pairs with you—a pair and a spare. If a pair breaks, the Peace Corps will replace them, using the information your doctor in the United States provided on the eyeglasses form during your examination. The Peace Corps discourages you from using contact lenses during your service to reduce your risk of developing a serious infection or other eye disease. Most Peace Corps countries do not have appropriate water and sanitation to support eye care with the use of contact lenses. The Peace Corps will not supply or replace contact lenses or associated solutions unless an ophthalmologist has recommended their use for a specific medical condition and the Peace Corps' Office of Medical Services has given approval.

If you are eligible for Medicare, are over 50 years of age, or have a health condition that may restrict your future participation in health care plans, you may wish to consult an insurance specialist about unique coverage needs before your departure. The Peace Corps will provide all necessary health care from the time you leave for your pre-departure orientation until you complete your service. When you finish, you will be entitled to the post-service health care benefits described in the Peace Corps *Volunteer Handbook*. You may wish to consider keeping an existing health plan in effect during your service if you think age or pre-existing conditions might prevent you from re-enrolling in your current plan when you return home.

Safety and Security—Our Partnership

Serving as a Volunteer overseas entails certain safety and security risks. Living and traveling in an unfamiliar environment, a limited understanding of the local language and culture, and the perception of being a wealthy American are some of the factors that can put a Volunteer at risk. Property theft and burglaries are not uncommon. Incidents of physical and sexual assault do occur, although almost all Volunteers complete their two years of service without serious personal safety problems.

Beyond knowing that Peace Corps approaches safety and security as a partnership with you, it might be helpful to see how this partnership works. Peace Corps has policies, procedures, and training in place to promote your safety. We depend on you to follow those policies and to put into practice what you have learned. An example of how this works in practice—in this case to help manage the risk of burglary—is:

- Peace Corps assesses the security environment where you will live and work
- Peace Corps inspects the house where you will live according to established security criteria
- Peace Corp provides you with resources to take measures such as installing new locks
- Peace Corps ensures you are welcomed by host country authorities in your new community

- Peace Corps responds to security concerns that you raise
- You lock your doors and windows
- You adopt a lifestyle appropriate to the community where you live
- You get to know neighbors
- You decide if purchasing personal articles insurance is appropriate for you
- You don't change residences before being authorized by Peace Corps
- You communicate concerns that you have to Peace Corps staff

This Welcome Book contains sections on: Living Conditions and Volunteer Lifestyle; Peace Corps Training; and Your Health Care and Safety that all include important safety and security information to help you understand this partnership. The Peace Corps makes every effort to give Volunteers the tools they need to function in the safest way possible, because working to maximize the safety and security of Volunteers is our highest priority. Not only do we provide you with training and tools to prepare for the unexpected, but we teach you to identify, reduce, and manage the risks you may encounter.

Factors that Contribute to Volunteer Risk
There are several factors that can heighten a Volunteer's risk, many of which are within the Volunteer's control. By far the most common crime that Volunteers experience is theft. Thefts often occur when Volunteers are away from their sites, in crowded locations (such as markets or on public transportation), and when leaving items unattended.

Before you depart for Ukraine there are several measures you can take to reduce your risk:

- Leave valuable objects in U.S.
- Leave copies of important documents and account numbers with someone you trust in the U.S.
- Purchase a hidden money pouch or "dummy" wallet as a decoy
- Purchase personal articles insurance

After you arrive in Ukraine, you will receive more detailed information about common crimes, factors that contribute to Volunteer risk, and local strategies to reduce that risk. For example, Volunteers in Ukraine learn to:

- Choose safe routes and times for travel, and travel with someone trusted by the community whenever possible

- Make sure one's personal appearance is respectful of local customs

- Avoid high-crime areas

- Know the local language to get help in an emergency

- Make friends with local people who are respected in the community

- Limit alcohol consumption

As you can see from this list, you must be willing to work hard and adapt your lifestyle to minimize the potential for being a target for crime. As with anywhere in the world, crime does exist in Ukraine. You can reduce your risk by avoiding situations that place you at risk and by taking precautions. Crime at the village or town level is less frequent than in the large cities; people know each other and generally are less likely to steal from their neighbors. Tourist attractions in large towns are favorite worksites for pickpockets.

The following are other security concerns in Ukraine of which you should be aware:

- **Robbery and burglary**. Volunteers in Ukraine have been burglarized in the past, so you will need to take the same precautions you would take in the United States to deter such incidents. The Peace Corps will cover the cost of installing new locks, security doors with peepholes, and window security devices if required.
- **Alcohol**. Unfortunately, some Volunteers in Ukraine have been robbed or assaulted while intoxicated. Intoxication decreases awareness and reaction time, leaving the intoxicated individual more vulnerable to predators. In addition, it is not uncommon to encounter intoxicated individuals while traveling on public transportation. During pre-service training, you will practice skills that are useful for identifying and avoiding situations related to alcohol use that can pose a threat to your personal safety.

- **Scams and fraud**. Because of the high incidence of credit card and ATM fraud, the U.S. Embassy strongly discourages the use of U.S. bank-issued credit cards and ATMs in Ukraine. Volunteers should exchange money at a bank and not with money exchanges near the bank, on the street, or with strangers. Volunteers have experienced various scams, and you will receive more information about potential scams during training and throughout your service.

While whistles and exclamations may be fairly common on the street, this behavior can be reduced if you dress conservatively, abide by local cultural norms, and respond according to the training you will receive.

Staying Safe: Don't Be a Target for Crime

You must be prepared to take on a large degree of responsibility for your own safety. You can make yourself less of a target, ensure that your home is secure, and develop relationships in your community that will make you an unlikely victim of crime. While the factors that contribute to your risk in Ukraine may be different, in many ways you can do what you would do if you moved to a new city anywhere: Be cautious, check things out, ask questions, learn about your neighborhood, know where the more risky locations are, use common sense, and be aware. You can reduce your vulnerability to crime by integrating into your community, learning the local language, acting responsibly, and abiding by Peace Corps policies and procedures. Serving safely and effectively in Ukraine will require that you accept some restrictions on your current lifestyle.

Volunteers attract a lot of attention both in large cities and at their sites, but they are likely to receive more negative attention in highly populated centers than at their sites, where "family," friends, and colleagues look out for them. While stares are fairly common on the street, this behavior can be reduced if you dress conservatively, avoid eye contact, and do not respond to unwanted attention. In addition, keep your money out of sight by using an undergarment money pouch that hangs around your neck and stays hidden under your shirt or inside your coat. Do not keep your money in outside pockets of backpacks, in coat pockets, or in fanny packs. And always walk with a companion at night. Female Volunteers should always ask someone they trust to walk them home. Having a male escort does not make you less independent, it makes you safer.

Support from Staff

If a trainee or Volunteer is the victim of a safety incident, Peace Corps staff is prepared to provide support. All Peace Corps posts have procedures in place to respond to incidents of crime committed against Volunteers. The first priority for all posts in the aftermath of an incident is to ensure the Volunteer is safe and receiving medical treatment as needed. After assuring the safety of the Volunteer, Peace Corps staff response may include reassessing the Volunteer's worksite and housing arrangements and making any adjustments, as needed. In some cases, the nature of the incident may necessitate a site or housing transfer. Peace Corps staff will also assist Volunteers with preserving their rights to pursue legal sanctions against the perpetrators of the crime. It is very important that Volunteers report incidents as they occur, not only to protect their peer Volunteers, but also to preserve the future right to prosecute. Should Volunteers decide later in the process that they want to proceed with the prosecution of their assailant, this option may no longer exist if the evidence of the event has not been preserved at the time of the incident.

Crime Data for Ukraine

Crime data and statistics for Ukraine, which is updated yearly, are available at the following link: http://www.peacecorps.gov/countrydata/ukraine

Please take the time to review this important information

Few Peace Corps Volunteers are victims of serious crimes and crimes that do occur overseas are investigated and prosecuted by local authorities through the local courts system. If you are the victim of a crime, you will decide if you wish to pursue prosecution. If you decide to prosecute, Peace Corps will be there to assist you. One of our tasks is to ensure you are fully informed of your options and understand how the local legal process works. Peace Corps will help you ensure your rights are protected to the fullest extent possible under the laws of the country.

If you are the victim of a serious crime, you will learn how to get to a safe location as quickly as possible and contact your Peace Corps office. It's important that you notify Peace Corps as soon as you can so Peace Corps can provide you with the help you need.

Volunteer Safety Support in Ukraine

The Peace Corps' approach to safety is a five-pronged plan to help you stay safe during your service and includes the following: information sharing, Volunteer training, site selection criteria, a detailed emergency action plan, and protocols for addressing safety and security incidents. Ukraine's in-country safety program is outlined below.

The Peace Corps/Ukraine office will keep you informed of any issues that may impact Volunteer safety through information sharing. Regular updates will be provided in Volunteer newsletters and in memorandums from the country director. In the event of a critical situation or emergency, you will be contacted through the emergency communication network. An important component of the capacity of Peace Corps to keep you informed is your buy-in to the partnership concept with the Peace Corps staff. It is expected that you will do your part in ensuring that Peace Corps staff members are kept apprised of your movements in-country so they are able to inform you.

Volunteer training will include sessions on specific safety and security issues in Ukraine. This training will prepare you to adopt a culturally appropriate lifestyle and exercise judgment that promotes safety and reduces risk in your home, at work, and while traveling. Safety training is offered throughout service and is integrated into the language, cross-cultural aspects, health, and other components of training. You will be expected to successfully complete all training competencies in a variety of areas, including safety and security, as a condition of service.

Certain site selection criteria are used to determine safe housing for Volunteers before their arrival. The Peace Corps staff works closely with host communities and counterpart agencies to help prepare them for a Volunteer's arrival and to establish expectations of their respective roles in supporting the Volunteer. Each site is inspected before the Volunteer's arrival to ensure placement in appropriate, safe, and secure housing and worksites. Site selection is based, in part, on any relevant site history; access to medical, banking, postal, and other essential services; availability of communications, transportation, and markets; different housing options and living arrangements; and other Volunteer support needs.

You will also learn about Peace Corps/Ukraine's detailed emergency action plan, which is implemented in the event of civil or political unrest or a natural disaster. When you arrive at your site, you will complete and submit a site locator form with your address, contact information, and a map to your house. If there is a security threat, you will gather with other Volunteers in Ukraine at predetermined locations until the situation is resolved or the Peace Corps decides to evacuate.

Finally, in order for the Peace Corps to be fully responsive to the needs of Volunteers, it is imperative that Volunteers immediately report any security incident to the Peace Corps office. The Peace Corps has established protocols for addressing safety and security incidents in a timely and appropriate manner, and it collects and evaluates safety and security data to track trends and develop strategies to minimize risks to future Volunteers.

DIVERSITY AND CROSS-CULTURAL ISSUES

In fulfilling its mandate to share the face of America with host countries, the Peace Corps is making special efforts to assure that all of America's richness is reflected in the Volunteer corps. More Americans of color are serving in today's Peace Corps than at any time in recent history. Differences in race, ethnic background, age, religion, and sexual orientation are expected and welcomed among our Volunteers. Part of the Peace Corps' mission is to help dispel any notion that Americans are all of one origin or race and to establish that each of us is as thoroughly American as the other despite our many differences.

Our diversity helps us accomplish that goal. In other ways, however, it poses challenges. In Ukraine, as in other Peace Corps host countries, Volunteers' behavior, lifestyle, background, and beliefs are judged in a cultural context very different from their own. Certain personal perspectives or characteristics commonly accepted in the United States may be quite uncommon, unacceptable, or even repressed in Ukraine.

Outside of Ukraine's capital, residents of rural communities have had relatively little direct exposure to other cultures, races, religions, and lifestyles. What people view as typical American behavior or norms may be a misconception, such as the belief that all Americans are rich and have blond hair and blue eyes. The people of Ukraine are justly known for their generous hospitality to foreigners; however, members of the community in which you will live may display a range of reactions to cultural differences that you present.

To ease the transition and adapt to life in Ukraine, you may need to make some temporary, yet fundamental compromises in how you present yourself as an American and as an individual. For example, female trainees and Volunteers may not be able to exercise the independence available to them in the United States; political discussions need to be handled with great care; and some of your personal beliefs may best remain undisclosed. You will need to develop techniques and personal strategies for coping with these and other limitations. The Peace Corps staff will lead diversity and sensitivity discussions during pre-service training and will be on call to provide support, but the challenge ultimately will be your own.

Overview of Diversity in Ukraine

The Peace Corps staff in Ukraine recognizes the adjustment issues that come with diversity and will endeavor to provide support and guidance. During pre-service training, several sessions will be held to discuss diversity and coping mechanisms. We look forward to having male and female Volunteers from a variety of races, ethnic groups, ages, religions, and sexual orientations, and hope that you will become part of a diverse group of Americans who take pride in supporting one another and demonstrating the richness of American culture.

What Might a Volunteer Face?

Possible Issues for Female Volunteers

Gender roles in Ukraine can be difficult to understand and accept. Ukrainian culture may appear to be discriminatory. Although men and women may receive equal pay for equal work, women are underrepresented in positions of power and often are not promoted as readily as men. These gender differences can present problems for Volunteers in job situations.

Volunteer Comments
—An issue for women in Ukraine is the overfriendliness of men under the influence of alcohol. Rather than attempting to be polite, women should simply walk away without giving them any attention. Other than Ukrainian men being more traditional in their views of a woman's ‚place' in society, which results in chivalrous behavior, men in Ukraine are quite respectful of women.

—Ukrainian streets are often unlit, as are stairwells and corridors, and in winter it gets dark before 5 p.m. I recommend that Volunteers always carry a flashlight and the personal alarm that the Peace Corps issues. Try not to be out alone after dark or, when that's impossible (e.g. in the winter), be home by the time most people come home from work. Get to know your neighbors. The old women sitting in front of the apartment buildings aren't just gossiping—they're unofficial door guards and they're watching out for you, too."
—For women, it is rare to see a Ukrainian female without makeup on, even when hiking! But they will know you are a foreigner anyway, so do what you normally would in terms of your style."

Possible Issues for Volunteers of Color

Racial and ethnic minorities in Ukraine—primarily Poles, Hungarians, Crimean Tatars, and Greeks—make up about 5 percent of the total population. Most Ukrainians have not had personal interactions with people of other races. They often assume that African-American or Asian-American Volunteers are university students from Africa or Asia rather than Americans. Thus,they may be stopped to show their identification papers more frequently than other Volunteers, particularly in larger cities where they are not known. On its website, the U.S. State Department now warns prospective travelers to Ukraine of ―increasing incidents of racially motivated violence.‖ In addition, a number of international human rights groups have expressed concern with the rise in ―skinhead‖ activity in big cities in Ukraine,

Volunteer Comments

―As a female African American serving in the Peace Corps/Ukraine community development program, my overall experience as a minority in Ukraine has been rewarding, challenging, and fulfilling. Nevertheless, every single person in cities other than Kyiv is likely to stare at you. And, as in any other country around the globe, you may encounter some racism in Ukraine. I have many Ukrainian friends and business acquaintances who treat me with respect and share the wonderful roots of Ukrainian culture. Ukrainians really get a kick out of an African-American woman speaking Ukrainian. People are amazed, and they love it.‖

―have not been treated differently by the general public or merchants because of my color. Nor can I recall any acts of discriminatory treatment related to the color of my skin.‖

Possible Issues for Senior Volunteers

Older people in Ukraine are generally respected and seen as sources of wisdom. They often have a greater degree of credibility upon arrival at their sites. The slow pace of change in Ukraine, however, may prove challenging for some individuals. In addition, certain conditions —uneven pavement, multistory buildings without elevators, and lack of amenities—combine to make life more demanding than in the United States.

Volunteer Comments

―Senior Volunteers are very well-respected, as are the Ukrainian seniors. Younger people offer me a seat on the trolley buses. The community respects my opinions partly because I am an American, but partly because I am over 55. Interaction among Volunteers of all ages is very acceptable."

—As a senior American woman with grandchildren, I have been asked frequently why I am here and not home with my family. Apparently, the senior women in Ukraine tend to be the caregivers for their grandchildren while their parents work, and they often live with their children."

—As a 60-year-old female Volunteer, I've got it better than anyone else in Ukraine. I don't have young folks' concerns and constraints; I don't face the issues that males face here; and, unlike many Ukrainians my age, I can eat properly and am in good health. I feel safe on the street, except for the potholes. So far, a dirty look from under my graying hair has been enough to avoid potential problems with other people. And developing friendships with Ukrainians of all ages has been an enjoyable process."

<u>Possible Issues for Gay, Lesbian, or Bisexual Volunteers</u>
Homosexuality was decriminalized in Ukraine in 1991. However, gays meet with much discrimination and civil rights abuses related to sexual orientation. Society generally views being gay, lesbian, or bisexual as abnormal. While networks of gays and lesbians are forming in some of the larger cities, gay life is hidden from the public and kept very discreet. Some gay and lesbian Volunteers in Ukraine have found that being open about their sexual orientation at their sites has had a negative impact on their effectiveness.

Volunteer Comment
—Although Ukrainians are becoming more open to discussing areas of sexuality, homosexuality is largely considered a deviation from the 'norm.' Though gay and bisexual singers and performers are currently in vogue, this is not indicative of the general opinion of the Ukrainian public. There are gay clubs and bars in at least two cities, including the capital, but these places are seedy products of an environment that does not allow people to express themselves freely."

<u>Possible Religious Issues for Volunteers</u>
Many Ukrainians have little knowledge of non-Christian faiths. There are Polish and Greek Catholic churches and Ukrainian Orthodox churches in

most communities. Most big cities have large numbers of Christian missionaries. Volunteers are sometimes mistaken for missionaries, and the Peace Corps is careful to maintain a separation from such groups. Please note, Volunteers cannot be placed in sites according to their religious beliefs.

Volunteer Comments
—Ask your rabbi about Ukraine and more than likely you will be told that some of the greatest scholars in Jewish history once lived here. Cities like Berdychiv, Zhytomyr, Uman, and many more were once home to primarily Jewish inhabitants, and their influence on the culture and food exists to this day. Since then, large numbers of Jews have left the country. There are a number of reasons for this, but it appears that most are looking for better economic opportunities or are reuniting with family."

—The question of anti-Semitism is raised by many Jewish Volunteers planning to serve in Ukraine. As in all parts of the world where Jews live, there are instances of anti-Semitism in Ukraine, but they are not common. Be assured that you can be open about your Jewish identity with Ukrainians; in almost all cases, they will be very accepting."

—Aside from the prevalent Orthodox and Catholic churches, there is a large Mormon presence in Ukraine and a fairly large Baptist presence. Many medium-sized cities have Jewish temples. For other faiths or denominations, the presence of churches drops significantly."

Possible Issues for Volunteers With Disabilities
As part of the medical clearance process, the Peace Corps Office of Medical Services determined that you were physically and emotionally capable, with or without reasonable accommodations, to perform a full tour of Volunteer service in Ukraine without unreasonable risk of harm to yourself or interruption of service. The Peace Corps/ Ukraine staff will work with disabled Volunteers to make reasonable accommodations for them in training, housing, jobsites, or other areas to enable them to serve safely and effectively.

As a disabled Volunteer in Ukraine, you may face a special set of challenges. In Ukraine, as in other parts of the world, some people hold prejudicial attitudes about individuals with disabilities and may discriminate against them. Also, there is very little of the infrastructure to accommodate individuals with disabilities that has been developed in the United States.

Possible Issues for Married Volunteers

Married Volunteers face a unique set of benefits and challenges during their service in Ukraine. Married PCVs often benefit from having a companion and friend at their site whom they trust. At the same time, it can be more difficult for married Volunteers to integrate into a community, as community members believe they are more independent and need more space. Married Volunteers should come to Ukraine prepared to reach out to their community to overcome any such perceptions.

Volunteer Comment
—‡lis harder to get involved in people's lives and families, I believe, when one is _older' and married. People think we are self-sufficient (although we have the same language problems as a single Volunteer), and hosting two people is very difficult for many Ukrainians because of space limitations."

FREQUENTLY ASKED QUESTIONS

How much luggage am I allowed to bring to Ukraine?
Most airlines have baggage size and weight limits and assess charges for transport of baggage that exceeds those limits. The Peace Corps has its own size and weight limits and will not pay the cost of transport for baggage that exceeds these limits. The Peace Corps' allowance is two checked pieces of luggage with combined dimensions of both pieces not to exceed 107 inches (length + width + height) and a carry-on bag with dimensions of no more than 45 inches. Checked baggage should not exceed 100 pounds total with a maximum weight of 50 pounds for any one bag.

Peace Corps Volunteers are not allowed to take pets, weapons, explosives, radio transmitters (shortwave radios are permitted), automobiles, or motorcycles to their overseas assignments. Do not pack flammable materials or liquids such as lighter fluid, cleaning solvents, hair spray, or aerosol containers. This is an important safety precaution.

What is the electric current in Ukraine?
The current is 220 volts, 50 cycles. Plugs and sockets are of the European two-pin type. If you bring 110-volt appliances, be sure to bring the appropriate transformers and adapters, which are not always easily available in Ukraine. Since hair dryers, irons, clocks, etc. are available here (some of which can be switched between 220 and 110 volts), you may want to leave your American appliances at home. However, the prices of name-brand items are generally higher than in the United States because of customs and import taxes. Electricity is sometimes rationed, so it is a good idea to bring items that can also run on batteries if necessary.

How much money should I bring?
Volunteers are expected to live at the same level as the people in their community. You will be given a settling-in allowance and a monthly living allowance, which should cover your expenses. Volunteers often wish to bring additional money for vacation travel to other countries. Credit cards and traveler's checks are preferable to cash. If you choose to bring extra money, bring the amount that will suit your own travel plans and needs.

When can I take vacation and have people visit me?
Each Volunteer accrues two vacation days per month of service (excluding training). Leave may not be taken during training, the first three months of service, or the last three months of service, except in conjunction with an authorized emergency leave. Family and friends are welcome to visit you after pre-service training and the first three months of service as long as their stay does not interfere with your work. Extended stays at your site are not encouraged and may require permission from your country director. The Peace Corps is not able to provide your visitors with visa, medical, or travel assistance.

Will my belongings be covered by insurance?
The Peace Corps does not provide insurance coverage for personal effects; Volunteers are ultimately responsible for the safekeeping of their personal belongings. However, you can purchase personal property insurance before you leave. If you wish, you may contact your own insurance company; additionally, insurance application forms will be provided, and we encourage you to consider them carefully. Volunteers should not ship or take valuable items overseas. Jewelry, watches, radios, cameras, and expensive appliances are subject to loss, theft, and breakage, and in many places, satisfactory maintenance and repair services are not available.

Do I need an international driver's license?
Volunteers in Ukraine do not need an international driver's license because they are prohibited from operating privately owned motorized vehicles. Most urban travel is by bus or taxi. Rural travel ranges from buses and minibuses to trucks, bicycles, and lots of walking. On very rare occasions, a Volunteer may be asked to drive a sponsor's vehicle, but this can occur only with prior written permission from the country director. Should this occur, the Volunteer may obtain a local driver's license. A U.S. driver's license will facilitate the process, so bring it with you just in case.

What should I bring as gifts for Ukraine friends and my host family?
This is not a requirement. A token of friendship is sufficient. Some gift suggestions include knickknacks for the house; pictures, books, or calendars of American scenes; souvenirs from your area; hard candies that will not melt or spoil; or photos to give away.

Where will my site assignment be when I finish training and how isolated will I be?

Peace Corps trainees are not assigned to individual sites until after they have completed pre-service training. This gives Peace Corps staff the opportunity to assess each trainee's technical and language skills prior to assigning sites, in addition to finalizing site selections with their ministry counterparts. If feasible, you may have the opportunity to provide input on your site preferences, including geographical location, distance from other Volunteers, and living conditions. However, keep in mind that many factors influence the site selection process and that the Peace Corps cannot guarantee placement where you would ideally like to be. Most Volunteers live in small towns or in rural villages and are usually within one hour from another Volunteer. Some sites require a 10- to 12-hour drive from the capital.

How can my family contact me in an emergency?

The Peace Corps' Counseling and Outreach Unit provides assistance in handling emergencies affecting trainees and Volunteers or their families. Before leaving the United States, instruct your family to notify the Office of Special Services immediately if an emergency arises, such as a serious illness or death of a family member. During normal business hours, the number for the Office of Special Services is 800.424.8580; select option 2, then extension 1470. After normal business hours and on weekends and holidays, the Special Services duty officer can be reached at the above number. For non-emergency questions, your family can get information from your country desk staff at the Peace Corps by calling 800.424.8580.

Can I call home from Ukraine?

Ukraine has good telephone connections with the United States, although service is most consistent from the capital and other large cities. Because international calls are very expensive, most Volunteers call home collect, establish a time to receive a call from home, or communicate via Skype.

Should I bring a cellular phone with me?

Ukraine has cellular phone service, and Peace Corps staff members are equipped with cellphones for daily operations. All Volunteers in Ukraine have cell phones. Differences in technology make most U.S. cellphones incompatible with Ukrainian systems, but Tri-band phones should work in Ukraine. You will need to have your cell phone company unlock your phone in the US, and while in Ukraine, you should purchase a local sim card.

Cellphones are available for purchase virtually everywhere, even in villages. Peace Corps will give you a special one-time allowance (about $30) to buy a cheap cellphone locally. Having a cellphone is both useful for safety reasons (especially when in remote areas) and also to keep in touch with fellow Volunteers, site colleagues, and Peace Corps staff while away from your site.

Will there be email and Internet access? Should I bring my computer?
Most Volunteers in Ukraine have access to e-mail, though access is not as consistent or fast as in the United States. Depending on where you live and work, you will be able to access e-mail at a local Internet cafe, at your place of work, from home (if you have a computer), or at the nearest regional center. Volunteers generally find the Internet to be the fastest and most affordable way to communicate with friends and family in the United States.

Most Volunteers bring laptop or tablet computers , but they are responsible for insuring and maintaining them. The Peace Corps will not replace stolen computers and strongly encourages those who bring them to get personal property insurance.

WELCOME LETTERS FROM UKRAINE VOLUNTEERS

I hardly know where to begin in attempting to convey the multifaceted and enriching experiences I have had as a Peace Corps Volunteer in Ukraine. When I first arrived as a trainee, I was full of hope and excitement. At the same time, I questioned if I had made the right decision in accepting my invitation to serve as a Volunteer teaching English as a foreign language (TEFL) in a country I knew so little about. I wondered what kind of impact I could make as a young American with no prior knowledge of Ukrainian or Russian. One year and seven months later, there is no doubt in my mind that joining the amazing network of over 300 PCVs in Ukraine was the right choice. In addition to finding a wide range of meaningful ways in which to serve and impact members of my community, my Ukrainian colleagues and friends have taught me invaluable lessons and helped me develop into a stronger, more knowledgeable member of the world community.

Before my departure for Peace Corps service, I tried to learn as much as I could about Ukraine via online research and by contacting currently serving Volunteers. The information and advice I obtained was helpful in packing and preparing mentally. For example, according to advice from PCVs, I decided to bring my laptop; it proved invaluable. However, remember to take all facts and guidance with a grain of salt. Ukraine is a very large country that differs significantly from east to west and from city to small village. Furthermore, as the pace of development increases, especially in large, metropolitan areas, everyday life continues to change. Not long ago, cellphones were a rarity; now at least half of the students at my school carry them to class and almost all PCVs purchase one not long after arrival.

As a TEFL Volunteer at a secondary school, one of my primary responsibilities is to teach conversational English.
In addition to these lessons, I have also taught business English, organized an English club, helped teach beginning English to kindergartners, and conducted teacher training for Ukrainian English teachers. These are just a few examples of the various ways in which Volunteers in Ukraine serve and become more involved members of their communities. With support from fellow PCVs and Peace Corps employees, the possibilities for impacting the course of development in Ukraine are endless.

While striving to make a positive contribution in Ukraine, I have found that my Ukrainian colleagues and the citizens of Ukraine, as a whole, have given me much more than I will ever be able to give back. They have taught me their language, culture, traditions, and history. They have supported and assisted me as a teacher, welcomed me into their communities, and provided inspiration in my work and everyday life. Each day of my service presents an opportunity to learn something new about my surroundings, myself, and the world. I can't imagine my life without Ukraine, and I am confident that my experience and the relationships I have built here will forever affect my outlook and the course of my life.

—Jessica Fisher

To be considering an invitation to Ukraine in the Peace Corps says a lot about what a fantastic and special person you are. It's not an easy decision to leave friends and family for over two years, but the benefits of living in Ukraine more than make up for being so far from home. The friendships you develop not only with fellow Peace Corps Volunteers, but also with the Ukrainian people, will last a lifetime.

When I left my first host family for my site there were tears in all our eyes. I still go and visit them and it feels like I am coming home when I do. But I can still remember that first night in their home. A strange bed in a strange country—all I could think of was: What have I done? I talked with the other PCVs in my training group and learned we all felt the same way. And we all quickly adapted to our new lives by helping each other and making sure we all communicated.

My site is a small town in southern Ukraine where I am the first Volunteer and the first American most of the townspeople have ever seen. I still get stared at when I walk through town, but it doesn't bother me anymore. There is so much to get used to when you settle in at your site. My second host family did a good job by introducing me to many of the shopkeepers, the post office lady, people at the phone company, etc., but there is so much they can't prepare you for—like living through one of the coldest winters in Ukraine without heat. You just keep adding layers, and when you go to sleep at night you roll yourself up in blankets like a tortilla. Even though the water pipes froze for five days and I was without running water, I had enough water stored in bottles to last for seven days. I still keep my backup water ready because the water is so inconsistent. It might sound shocking to you to live this way, but this is my world and right now I wouldn't trade it for anything. Just when I get to the point of wanting to scream, one of my students comes up and gives me a hug, or a flower, or a chocolate, or just says thank you, and I am ready to keep going.

Whenever I get down, and believe me it happens to everyone, I use my cellphone to text another PCV. A cellphone here is a necessity for your mental stability! My town feels so isolated, and that is the hardest part about living in Ukraine. Transportation is very difficult here, but you learn to adapt and make sure you get on the bus! Every few months, I travel to the Oblast capital of Kherson to take part in ‐retail therapy," and that refreshes and restores me. I ask myself after living here and going through the hardships, would I do it again? My answer is: in a heartbeat! Being a senior Volunteer I thought I knew myself well, but I have uncovered parts of me I never knew existed. My mantra is whatever doesn't kill me only makes me stronger and I plan on leaving Ukraine an extremely strong person!

—Denice Dunkerley

I can recall a time in the not-so-distant past when I learned of my invitation to serve in Peace Corps/Ukraine. I immediately jumped at the opportunity, only vaguely aware of the country's recent history as it lurched through its transition to a market-based economy. I suddenly found myself with an insatiable curiosity to absorb as much as possible about the culture, the history, and the people that make Ukraine so unique, consuming as much information as I could. In spite of my enthusiasm and best intentions, no amount of research could actually prepare me for what I would witness and experience in Ukraine during the next two years.

I viewed everything at first with bewildered awe, with eyes wide open at the novelty of my surroundings. It seemed so exotic. The Cyrillic alphabet itself was a curiosity, providing little moments of satisfaction when I was able to successfully decode a word on a billboard or storefront. The challenges posed by my new surroundings heightened my sense of self-awareness, as well as an acute awareness of the cultural differences between Americans and Ukrainians. Through my host family, and numerous other Ukrainians who accepted us into their community during training, I experienced a feeling of hospitality and warmth that I would later come to understand as one of the defining aspects of Slavic culture. My experiences during training underscored the importance Ukrainians placed on community, and how vital it would be for my success and happiness over the next two years to discover my own sense of community.

I began building relationships with the people who would come to mean so much to me immediately upon arriving at my site. My colleagues at the small business development center in rural Crimea were not only eager to welcome me into their workplace, but also into their hearts and minds. What I received over the next two years was an up-close-and-personal look at the culture of the Crimean Tatars, the descendants of the original inhabitants of the peninsula. Living and working among an ethnic minority in a largely homogenous Slavic culture provided innumerable opportunities to see and experience a very unique side of Ukraine. At times, it felt as though I was serving in Peace Corps/Uzbekistan—the nuances of tradition, language, food, religion, and history all very divergent from the rest of the country. Every Volunteer's experience is something uniquely personal to the individual, and I came to appreciate what a tremendous opportunity I had been given to understand more about human diversity. In the process, I came to learn so much more about myself.

Sure, the work was not without its challenges, with many false starts and ideas that never quite came to fruition. Such shortcomings only make the successes feel that much sweeter when they ultimately do arrive. I feel accomplished in having worked with members of a small community to adopt a planning mindset and begin taking steps to bettering their own livelihoods.

The best piece of advice I received during my service was also the most simple. Early on, I was told by my country director, "Ukraine is going to happen." It took nearly half of my service until the true meaning of this statement became deeply understood. The top-level forces at work are so powerful and dynamic, and the rapid changes they bring with them are almost beyond comprehension for us and many Ukrainians. There is only so much one individual can influence. Finally understanding this, I arrived at a point where I simply let go—where I stopped grasping, and where I allowed everything in my surroundings to flow through me. Suddenly, things that once seemed to cause great anxiety ceased to be a disturbance. I found myself no longer translating what was said to me, but really being able to communicate in a meaningful way. In the end, it is people that make Peace Corps go. Learning how to open ourselves up and truly appreciate our human likenesses—our hopes, desires, fears—and not our differences is perhaps the most crucial take-away point from my entire Peace Corps experience.

Ukraine is going to happen. It is a fascinating country rich with history, culture, and tradition, and is well along on its own unique trajectory of development. I feel incredibly fortunate to have served here during a time of such great political, economic, and social transition. It is important to understand the paradoxical goal of international development—to put ourselves out of a job. Realize that Peace Corps will not always be here, and seize the moment that is provided to you.

—Michael Kreidler

My husband and I serve as community development volunteers in Vinnytsia. We are older Volunteers. It was our desire when we were young to join the Peace Corps, but jobs, family, mortgages, etc. got in our way. So now we are living our dream here in Ukraine. If you choose to join the Peace Corps, you will embark on the adventure of a lifetime. It comes with a mix of emotions that are exciting, scary, wonderful, depressing, rewarding, confusing, and more.

During Peace Corps training, which was the hardest part for us, you will be given lots of good advice and encouragement, as well as useful information. Training will provide you with the knowledge to live and carry out your responsibilities while in Ukraine. Every day will bring a new experience that you know friends back home just would not believe or be able to understand. You will return to America a better American. You will learn what a great country we have, and how we must strive each day to defend the rights our Constitution provides.

Freedom of speech will take on a new meaning. You will realize that you are no longer in Kansas, Dorothy, but are in a different culture with different ways of life and of doing things. You will learn that they are not wrong, but just different. You will learn just how America is viewed from afar and be proud. You will learn that life can be simpler and just as great. We learned from our host family of five that you can survive with two knives, one sharp and one for spreading. You will learn to trust yourself to be entertained. There will be days during which you will cry because you miss home and family. You will learn to deal with loneliness and to make friends with people who do not share your culture. You will learn to handle your frustrations and anger when there is no one else to listen. This and many more lessons are waiting for you if you choose this path. Sometimes it is a hurry-up-and-wait kind of situation with the Peace Corps, but you will never meet such great people as your new friends in the Peace Corps. We know that some of the people we have met here will be part of our lives from now on.

We always thought of Peace Corps Volunteers being in Africa, South America, Pacific countries, and Latin America, but not part of the former Soviet Union. We never dreamed that we would be here in Ukraine. We never dreamed we would even travel to this part of the world. We cannot wait for you to experience the architecture of the onion domes, the flocks of geese, the horse-drawn carts, the bazaar in summer when all the vegetables are in and the smell is incredible, meeting people who have never met an American before, and many other adventures. The most important thing is the real American inside of you that is just waiting to come out.

The decision is yours and you must give consideration to your family, your relationships, your financial situation, your career, your health—but also your dreams.

—Elene Hertweck

PACKING LIST

This list has been compiled by Volunteers serving in Ukraine and is based on their experience. Use it as an informal guide in making your own list, bearing in mind that each experience is individual. There is no perfect list! You obviously cannot bring everything on the list, so consider those items that make the most sense to you personally and professionally. You can always have things sent to you later. As you decide what to bring, keep in mind that you have an 80-pound weight limit on baggage. And remember, you can get almost everything you need in Ukraine.

Before you move to your site, the Peace Corps will provide you with a space heater, fire extinguisher, smoke detector, many technical resources and language manuals, and a medical kit (described in an earlier section of this book).

Your living allowance should not be considered a source of funding for major clothing purchases, although replacement clothing is factored into the living allowance. The Peace Corps does not provide reimbursement for winter clothing purchased in the United States. The hard water and strong detergent, not to mention hand-washing, will be harsh on your clothing, so make sure that whatever you bring can stand up to this treatment. Most Volunteers wear their clothes for several days before washing them, so dark colors are a good idea. It gets cold in the winter, so pack for any winter weather. Jeans, khakis, and slacks offer very little value in terms of warmth, so men and women alike should bring a few pairs of thermal underwear. Bring clothes that do not require frequent and special care (i.e., dry cleaning). Blazers, suits, sport coats, and sweaters should be in dark colors to disguise the toil of frequent use. Remember, too, that you will likely be laundering your clothes by hand – jeans, light-colored clothing, and other fabrics can prove difficult to wash, dry, and keep their color in these conditions. A wide variety of clothes is available here, but quality can be lacking. If you have a hard time finding your size in the United States, you won't find it here, and genuine ‐high-tech" fibers are not readily available. Very warm, locally-made winter clothes can be purchased in-country. Walking will be your main mode of transportation around town, and the terrain here is rather rugged, so you need footwear that can take a lot of abuse.

Dress is very important in Ukraine. The popular image of a Peace Corps Volunteer in sandals and a T-shirt with a university logo is not appropriate in this country (nor is military-style clothing or accessories). Fair or not, people are judged by the way they dress in Ukraine, more so than what you may be used to in the United States. Your colleagues will dress as professionals and for you to do otherwise will be considered disrespectful. If you come to work inappropriately dressed, your colleagues, students, and others in the community will probably not say anything to you directly but may talk unfavorably about you to others. Following the lead of your co-workers will help you gain acceptance and respect in your community. This does not mean that you need to spend a lot of money on new clothing. Rather, be selective in what you bring, and consider buying some of your professional clothing in Ukraine. The quality and style may not be equal to American brands, but they are the same clothes your local colleagues will be wearing. Luggage should be lightweight, durable, lockable, and easy to carry. Duffel bags and backpacks without frames are best because you will be hauling your luggage around on foot—there are no redcaps or luggage carts in this part of the world.

General Clothing
Bring comfortable, professional-looking clothes that are appropriate for many occasions and can be layered according to the weather. (Note that you are expected to dress professionally during training.) Because you may be wearing the same clothes for two years, quality is more important than quantity. It is culturally acceptable in Ukraine to have a small wardrobe, so do not over-pack. Clothes should be wrinkle-fee (polyester-cotton blends are recommended), easy to clean, and dark-colored (you are likely to be washing your clothes by hand and cleaning whites is a chore. Likewise, wringing out clothes in the washing process, such as jeans, can be very tedious!). It is possible to buy clothes in Ukraine, but selection and sizes are limited. One option is to have clothes custom-made, which is not as costly as it is in the United States.

Specific clothing recommendations include the following:
- Trench coat for spring and fall and possibly a light jacket
- Full-length winter coat or parka with lining (down is recommended)
- Mix-or-match clothes for layering, such as solid-color turtlenecks
- Lightweight and heavyweight sweaters

- Gloves or mittens, preferably wool; glove liners are nice, too (and available locally)
- Hats (even if your head isn't cold, the babushkas will make you wear a hat)
- Long thermal underwear (cotton or silk)
- Wool or Lycra-wool blend socks
- Casual clothes: jeans, walking shorts, T-shirts, turtlenecks
- Bathing suit
- Sports and fitness clothing, such as jogging pants (shorts are inappropriate in most places but can be worn in a gym or when running in a stadium)

For Men
- One suit for professional occasions
- Slacks for business casual wear; in most cases, khakis or cords with a blazer and tie are acceptable in schools and universities
- Shirts for professional wear
- Jackets
- Ties

For Women
- One suit for professional occasions
- Variety of slacks for different seasons
- Blouses
- Durable stockings (available in Ukraine, though not in all sizes)
- Your usual accessories

Shoes
- Comfortable and durable work shoes (you will be doing a lot of walking), which are not easy to find in Ukraine
- Warm, waterproof boots that are dressy enough to wear with work clothes and large enough to wear with warm socks (although boots are available in Ukraine, large sizes for women may be difficult to find)
- Heavy-duty sandals (e.g., Tevas)
- Athletic shoes
- Slippers (you will wear these alot, as Ukrainians remove their shoes as soon as they walk in the door)

- Traction aids (e.g., Yaktrax); useful because walking on slippery roads in winter may be challenging, as it increases risk of falls and traumatic injuries when walking on ice; traction aids will help you feel confident and safe when walking on ice

Personal Hygiene and Toiletry Items

Unless you have to have specific brands, you can get almost everything you need—e.g., shampoo, conditioner, lotion, shaving cream, toothpaste, antiperspirant, hair spray, coloring products, razors—in Ukraine. Things to consider bringing:

- Two pairs of eyeglasses, if you wear them; also consider bringing a repair kit
- Two-year supply of contact lens solutions (the Peace Corps does not provide supplies for contacts)
- Three-month supply of any prescription medication you take
- Makeup (also available in Ukraine if you are not particular about brands)
- Start-up supply of feminine hygiene products (widely available in stores, bazaars, and kiosks, but it may take some time to determine where to get what you want)
- Moisturizing hand cream (also available in Ukraine)
- Hand sanitizer that does not require water (also available in Ukraine)
- Foot aids such as pads for corns, if you have tender feet
- Spot remover or Woolite (for clothes that need special care)
- Fabric refresher or odor remover (e.g., Febreeze)
- Tweezers
- Nail clipper or emery boards
- Dental floss (also available in Ukraine)
- 3 month supply of vitamins or supplements (the Peace Corps provides multivitamins after training)

Kitchen

You can easily buy most kitchen supplies in Ukraine. There are a few items, however, that you might consider bringing:

- Basic cookbook (bring a vegetarian cookbook if you prefer vegetarian dishes); a cookbook of dishes that can be prepared from locally available products will be provided to you
- Favorite recipes

- Measuring cups and spoons with both metric and nonmetric markings
- Oven thermometer
- Good vegetable peeler
- Artificial sweetener (sugar and honey are available)
- Twist ties
- Plastic storage bags (one-quart and one-gallon freezer bags are best)
- Favorite seasonings, such as Tabasco sauce, vanilla, Old Bay, cloves, taco spices, cumin, cayenne pepper, and chili powder (many basic spices are available locally)
- Favorite foods, such as chocolate chips, peanut butter, maple syrup, popcorn, and gravy and salad dressing mixes

Miscellaneous

- Favorite music, movies and workout videos
- Shortwave radio for international news
- MP3 player, thumb drive
- Laptop computer with a good surge protector; if you bring one, be sure to insure it
- Digital camera
- Medium-sized daypack for weekend travel
- Sturdy water bottle
- Umbrella (available in Ukraine)
- Durable, water-resistant, and inexpensive watch, with an alarm if possible; an extra battery is also useful
- Reliable alarm clock that runs without electricity
- Small but powerful flashlight, perhaps one that attaches to a key chain (can be bought in Ukraine)
- Neck safe or money belt (it is safest to carry your money and passport on your person)
- Sewing kit (with safety pins)
- Sleeping bag with stuff sack for traveling in cold weather
- Fleece throw/lap blanket for cold nights
- Musical instruments (if you play)
- Bring copies of all financial and personal documents, such as a Power of Attorney, university transcripts and/or diplomas, birth certificates, passport, and credit cards

- Graduate study materials (e.g., GRE, LSAT), as applicable
- A few books by your favorite authors or an e-book
- Appliances—buying them locally may eliminate the need to bring a voltage converter; items such as irons, blow dryers, and stereos are available at reasonable prices
- Teaching materials (for education Volunteers), such as markers, chalk, erasers, magazines, simple children's books, and American music; you can also pack items for someone to ship to you later
- Interesting wall decorations (maps, posters, etc.)
- Swiss Army knife with corkscrew or Leatherman tool (very useful)
- Duct tape (can be used for all sorts of things)
- Photos of home to show your host family, students, friends, and colleagues (These provide a great introduction for your host family and online photos most likely won't be possible when you first arrive to Ukraine.)
- Games such as Scrabble, cards, Frisbee, Uno, Nerf football
- Quick-drying travel towel (available at www.rei.com) and washcloths
- Day planner
- Dictionary (although the Peace Corps will give you one)
- Suntan lotion (selection of brands here is limited)
- Note cards and greeting cards

PRE-DEPARTURE CHECKLIST

The following list consists of suggestions for you to consider as you prepare to live outside the United States for two years. Not all items will be relevant to everyone, and the list does not include everything you should make arrangements for.

Family

- Notify family that they can call the Peace Corps' Office of Special Services at any time if there is a critical illness or death of a family member (24-hour telephone number: 800.424.8580, extension 1470).

- Give the Peace Corps' *On the Home Front* handbook to family and friends.

Passport/Travel

- Forward to the Peace Corps travel office all paperwork for the Peace Corps passport and visas.

- Verify that your luggage meets the size and weight limits for international travel.

- Obtain a personal passport if you plan to travel after your service ends. (Your Peace Corps passport will expire three months after you finish your service, so if you plan to travel longer, you will need a regular passport.)

Medical/Health

- Complete any needed dental and medical work.

- If you wear glasses, bring two pairs.

- Arrange to bring a three-month supply of all medications (including birth control pills) you are currently taking.

Insurance

- Make arrangements to maintain life insurance coverage.

- Arrange to maintain supplemental health coverage while you are away. (Even though the Peace Corps is responsible for your health care during Peace Corps service overseas, it is advisable for people who have pre-existing conditions to arrange for the continuation of their supplemental health coverage. If there is a lapse in coverage, it is often difficult and expensive to be reinstated.)

- Arrange to continue Medicare coverage if applicable.

Personal Papers

- Bring a copy of your certificate of marriage or divorce.

Voting

- Register to vote in the state of your home of record. (Many state universities consider voting and payment of state taxes as evidence of residence in that state.)

- Obtain a voter registration card and take it with you overseas.

- Arrange to have an absentee ballot forwarded to you overseas.

Personal Effects
- Purchase personal property insurance to extend from the time you leave your home for service overseas until the time you complete your service and return to the United States.

Financial Management
- Keep a bank account in your name in the U.S.

- Obtain student loan deferment forms from the lender or loan service.

- Execute a Power of Attorney for the management of your property and business.

- Arrange for deductions from your readjustment allowance to pay alimony, child support, and other debts through the Office of Volunteer Financial Operations at 800.424.8580, extension 1770.

- Place all important papers—mortgages, deeds, stocks, and bonds—in a safe deposit box or with an attorney or other caretaker.

CONTACTING PEACE CORPS HEADQUARTERS

This list of numbers will help connect you with the appropriate office at Peace Corps headquarters to answer various questions. You can use the toll-free number and extension or dial directly using the local numbers provided. Be sure to leave the toll-free number and extensions with your family so they can contact you in the event of an emergency.

Peace Corps Headquarters
Toll-free Number: 800.424.8580, Press 2, and then
                                        Ext. # (see below)

Peace Corps' Mailing Address:

                                        Peace Corps
                                        Paul D. Coverdell Peace Corps Headquarters
                                        1111 20th Street, NW
                                        Washington, DC 20526

For Questions About:	Staff	Toll-free Extension	Direct/ Local Number
Responding to an Invitation	Office of Placement	Ext. 1840	202.692.1840
Programming or Country Information	Desk Officer Email: Ukraine@ peacecorps.gov		202.692.2422

For Questions About:	Staff	Toll-free Extension	Direct/ Local Number
Plane Tickets, Passports, Visas, or Other Travel Matters	Travel Officer (Sato Travel)	Ext. 1170	202.692.1170
Legal Clearance	Office of Placement	Ext. 1845	202.692.1845
Medical Clearance and Forms Processing (including dental)	Screening Nurse	Ext. 1500	202.692.1500
Medical Reimbursements	Handled by a Subcontractor		800.818.8772
Loan Deferments, Taxes, Readjustment Allowance Withdrawals, Power of Attorney	Volunteer Financial Operations	Ext. 1770	202.692.1770
Staging (Pre-departure Orientation) and Reporting Instructions	Office of Staging	Ext. 1865	202.692.1865

Note: You will receive comprehensive information (hotel and flight arrangements) three to five weeks before departure. This information is not available sooner.

Family Emergencies (to get information to a Volunteer overseas)	Office of Special Services	Ext. 1470 *(24 hours)*	202.692.1470